3 Steps

to

Better Relationships

Improve ANY Relationship Using These 3 Easy Steps

May all your Relationships be Radiant!

TRENT JANISCH

Thank you for purchasing this book.

For more works by Trent Janisch,

please visit

www.trentjanisch.com

3 Steps

to

Better Relationships

Improve ANY Relationship Using These 3 Easy Steps

by

TRENT JANISCH

www.trentjanisch.com

ISBN: 978-0-9936921-1-6

The Power You Are Publishing

Suite 282

22-2475 Dobbin Rd

West Kelowna, British Columbia V4T 2E9

CANADA

DISCLAIMER

The author of this book does not issue medical advice or prescribe the use of any technique as a form of treatment for physical, emotional, or medical conditions of any sort. Please seek out the advice of a licensed physician for any treatment. The author's intention is to provide information of a general nature for your consideration to help you in your progress toward your greater emotional and spiritual well-being. By deciding to exercise your right to act upon any information in this book, you agree to accept full responsibility for your actions and any ensuing consequences and release the author and publisher of this book from any liability. The author and publisher of this book neither assume nor accept any responsibility for your actions.

DEDICATION

To Jasmin and Saje.

You have been, and continue to be, two of my greatest teachers in the meaning of Relationship. Thank you for all that we share in life.

I love you.

TABLE OF CONTENTS

Think
about
this...

*"Your **presence** (mood) is like a water source your friends and family drink from. Ask yourself, are you nourishing them or poisoning them?"*

- Trent Janisch

IT'S SO IMPORTANT FOR YOU TO ACTUALLY PRACTICE THESE 3 STEPS

It is often said that the quality of your life is determined by the quality of your relationships.

There is great wisdom in this phrase.

When you take a moment and think about it, you will find that everything you have in your life came to you by way of your connections with others - your *relationships*.

The people in your life are the primary environment in which you live. Your relationships, then, are like a garden that provides you with most everything you need to enjoy your life.

As your relationships improve, so does the quality of your life.

So, how is the quality of your life today?

Could it be a little bit better?

What would you like to have **more** of in your life right now?

What would you like **less** of?

Actually think about this for a moment...

Why I Wrote This Book

It makes me sad to see people needlessly suffer every day in different areas of their lives, all because of poor relationship/communication skills.

I see couples divorce and their families being torn apart when all they needed was to cultivate a safe environment in which they could openly share their real feelings and needs with each other.

I see talented people just scraping by financially when they could be communicating their value more effectively or, in some cases, just getting along better with other people.

I wrote this book to help you avoid any needless future grief by sharing the very **root** of what makes relationships work and how to make them work for you.

You deserve to have the right tools at hand; tools that can improve **any** area of your life.

Knowing how to cultivate good relationships is the real secret to getting more of what you want in life. As you develop better relationship skills, you become a really good 'Life Gardener' - someone who grows the Life experiences they desire.

Learning to to do this will take some time and practice. And one thing I know is, you will only invest the time to *consistently practice* the 3 Steps shared in this book when you actually believe your investment is worth it.

For this reason, let's begin with a little story...

A Tale of Two Lumberjacks

In the days before chainsaws, Jim and Ed, two young lumberjacks, set out into the nearby forest to cut down their daily quota of trees for the local sawmill.

Jim walked through the forest with Ed in silence. He had an air of determination about him that Ed hadn't noticed before. It had been 4 years now that Jim and his wife, Marie, had been trying to start a family. Having almost lost all hope, the couple were now miraculously expecting their first child. More than ever, Jim was now determined to work even harder to support his growing family.

As the two men came up on Whitetail Creek, Jim finally broke his silence. "I'll take these trees here off to the right, Ed. You go further down the trail and I'll see you at lunchtime". "Alright, Jim", Ed replied and, without stopping, he carried on northeast toward his destination.

Ed Harman was a thickset man standing 6 foot 4 inches and weighing in at 245 pounds. Ed dearly loved the forest and his work was, for him, a passion. He knew just where and how to cut any size tree and could land it on a dime. Within minutes, Ed was hard at work chopping down his first prize of the day.

Lunchtime arrived sooner than Ed expected and he had already fallen two towering Douglas Firs. He grabbed his pack and began the short hike back up the wildlife trail toward Jim to have their lunch together.

Ed found Jim right where he'd left him. Jim was feverishly chopping at a huge Redwood still looming over the forest.

Ed noticed this was still Jim's first tree. It had been hours and Jim was still frantically chopping. Ed called out, "Jim! JIM!! It's time for lunch. Take a break!".

Jim stopped working for a moment to wipe his brow and replied, "I can't, Ed. I don't have time.".

"Is this still your first tree?" Ed asked.

"Yes", Jim replied, "that's why I can't break for lunch yet. I want to get this tree down. You go ahead and eat".

Ed shook his head and asked another question, "Jim, why don't you sharpen your axe?"

Stressed and agitated, Jim snapped back, "I TOLD YOU, ED! I DON"T HAVE TIME!".

The Moral of The Story

It may seem obvious to you that if Jim invested the time in sharpening his axe, he would have a much easier task of chopping down his trees. Jim would get more work done in less time. He would earn more money and have more free time to spend with his family.

The fact that Jim was stressed kept him blind to the benefits of taking a break. He felt there was no time to sharpen his axe even though it would make his work easier and ultimately enhance the quality of his life.

Sometimes it seems hard to make time for what's important because of the stress caused by so many things competing for your attention. If you are feeling overwhelmed, take some time to relax and assess what's important to you. If it really is important, you'll find it's worth making time for.

Take a moment now.

How important are your relationships in life?

Believe it or not, your relationships are to you what those trees were to Jim - a livelihood.

Everything you have in your life comes to you by way of your relationships.

Your relationship skill-set is your axe.

This book is the stone that can sharpen your axe.

It's now up to you to sharpen it.

HEALTHY RELATIONSHIPS ARE YOUR PERSONAL GOLDMINE

Think about this:

Everything you want in life depends on the existence of other people.

For example, ask yourself, "Where does my money come from?".

Whether you are an employee or a business owner, you'll find your money comes to you through other people.

In order to earn money, you must find and develop relationships with people who are willing to pay you for your product or service.

These relationships are the key to your income.

As you improve your ability to connect with others, you can begin to increase your abundance.

More Than Money

In addition to Money, your quality of life also includes the areas of Love & Friendship, Spirit, Health, and Time Freedom. Each of these areas is directly dependent upon the state of your relationships with others.

Love & Friendship

Sharing time with the people you love is what makes life fun and worth living.

While periods of solitude have their benefits, being disconnected from others for too long can be a recipe for loneliness, depression, and even mental instability.

You have needs that you either *cannot* or *choose not* to fulfill on your own.

Because of this, your existence gives purpose to other people's lives - by helping fulfill your needs, their actions take on a purpose.

Other people give purpose to your life for this same reason - fulfilling their needs give your actions a purpose.

From this perspective, it would seem that we exist to serve one another and <u>we</u> are each other's reason for being.

Knowing how to deepen your connection with others strengthens your sense of purpose, fulfillment and your ability to truly live with passion.

<u>Health</u>

Improved relationships are strengthened connections that bring about greater levels of trust. When you really trust someone, when you know you can rely on them, you feel safe with them. This feeling of safety sets into motion what Dr. Herbert Benson of Harvard Medical School calls the "Relaxation Response".

The 'Relaxation Response' is the name given to a neurological/biochemical event in your body that is the opposite of your 'Stress Response'.

During times of perceived safety, your parasympathetic nervous system is activated and your body sets about making repairs, increasing digestion, breathing more deeply, and building up the immune system. In other words, it boosts your overall health.

For this reason, the more relationships in your life in which you cultivate trust, the safer you perceive your environment to be, and the healthier you become. So, one of the best things you can do for your Health long-term is to cultivate a life filled with trusting relationships.

Time Freedom

In our 'uber-busy' world, people often complain about not having enough time in a day. This is really odd from the perspective that, for as long as we can recall, there has only ever been 24 hours in a day. What is it we need more time for?

The truth is, we don't need more time in a day, we need more clarity around what is truly important to us. Here it's essential for us to, first, be in touch with our deepest values and then make decisions from this values-based reference point.

You automatically make time for what you believe is important to you.

When you know your deepest values and must decide which tasks are most important for you to invest your time in, consider these two points:

1) Your most important tasks are actions that affect your life long-term.

2) Your most important tasks are things that only you can do - i.e. if you don't do them, they don't get done.

Sometimes, tasks which only you can do will require more time to complete than was originally scheduled. This is an indication that the original time allotted for the task was unrealistic. When this happens, your ability to effectively communicate with others is essential for either coming up with deadline extensions or collaborative solutions.

Here, your success relies upon your ability to cultivate trust and understanding.

For all those other tasks that don't specifically need you to be the one to perform them, your relationship skills will pay off here in finding good people to delegate to. Once again, your free time is reliant upon your ability to cultivate trust and communicate effectively.

What You Get

In this book, I'm sharing 3 simple steps that you can apply today to begin enhancing the quality of any relationship with another person. As you consistently apply these 3 steps with everyone, you will strengthen the bonds that enable you to enhance your lifestyle in any of the areas mentioned above.

However, simply knowing these 3 steps cannot change your life.

To create the most positive change, you must *consistently apply* them.

I suggest you start small and begin with just one person. Make it fun and be curious to see what happens when you actively apply these steps.

Practice this process and make these *3 Steps* a HABIT. When you do, you will have automated the process of creating and sustaining the environment that supports you in growing a richer, happier life.

-3-
WHERE YOU BEGIN

Whenever you decide to change anything about your life, it is important to have a good overview of exactly what it is you are doing, keeping in mind that real change can only occur when the conditions are right.

You are about to discover 3 things you can do together to enhance the quality of your life. Think of these 3 things as seeds that you will plant into your garden.

In order for these 3 seeds to properly take root and grow, you must ensure that these seeds are planted in the right environment. Your first job, then, is to create the right environmental conditions.

Preparing the Soil

Did you know a vegetable farmer doesn't grow vegetables? The vegetables actually grow on their own. It's the Farmer's job to create and maintain the right environmental conditions for those vegetables to grow.

The same principle applies here. Before making any change in your behaviour, it is vitally important that you first create the right conditions to support your new way of being.

You must create the right inner environment that supports the 3 steps you are about to learn in this book. The right inner environment is the mindset that comes about as a result of the right "Why" question.

This question is:

"Why do we have relationships?"

When you were born, you were born into relationship with the world around you and the people in it. Have you ever really consciously thought about why you have relationships in the first place?

It's because you can't live without them.

This reliance we have upon one another is called *Interdependence*.

Recognizing the important role that *Interdependence* plays in your life is key to success in your relationships.

INTERDEPENDENCE :
YOUR MINDSET OF SUCCESS

'Relationship' is the word used to represent

the way in which you are connected with the
world around you. In the beginning, you
needed a sympathetic connection with your
parents in order for them to care for you.
Without this connection you would not have
survived.

Even when you are seemingly independent and
taking care of yourself, you still rely on others
to survive. You need home-builders to provide
you with a house or apartment; customers to
give you money for the product/service you
provide; people to grow the food you eat:
truckers to transport food to the supermarket;
furniture makers to provide your furniture,
health-care providers and so on. In order to

enjoy any sort of life, we all need each other. We provide each other with what we cannot provide for ourselves.

Interdependence is the environment that supports your independence.

Everything is Connected

On a grander scale, you need rich soil to grow your food. You need trees and algae to provide you with oxygen. You need fresh water to drink. You are in relationship with (connected with) the planet and everything upon it. Everything is interconnected and affects everything else - either directly or indirectly. Nothing is insignificant. We are all part of this ONE body we call "LIFE".

Nature's Balance is the governing/organizing force of LIFE. We are each part of this balance which consists of the way in which all things provide for each other.

If something didn't serve the balance of Nature, it would not exist.

You exist for a reason - you are part of the Balance of Nature. Your presence makes a difference.

The moment you decide to own the difference you make in the world around you is the moment you begin to take control over the quality of your life.

Your relationships are your connections with LIFE. These connections feed you and sustain you. By improving your connections with LIFE (everything around you), you improve the quality of your life.

- 5 -

THE FUNDAMENTAL HUMAN NEED

At the core of your being is the fundamental 'need' to be Heard; to be Seen; to be Felt; to be Understood; to be Recognized and Acknowledged. Fundamentally, you need to know that you are in some way valuable to the world around you because your survival depends on it. This fundamental human need is hardwired into your brain and nervous system as part of your body's Survival Instinct.

Needs & Fears

The word 'need' represents the idea of something we cannot live without. But 'need' is just one side of a coin. On the other side of this coin is a different word that travels with 'need' wherever it goes. This word is 'fear'.

Whenever you notice the word 'need', remember, it is tied to a 'fear'. 'Need' and 'fear' go hand-in-hand.

For example, if you believe you need water to survive, you are afraid to be without it for too long. The same is true for any other 'need'.

Because all people share the basic need to be seen and heard, we also share the same basic fear of being ignored, abandoned, or rejected. We are born with the intuitive understanding that we need the world around us in order to survive. So, as far as your inner Survival Instinct is concerned, if your surroundings abandon/reject/ignore you, it poses a threat to your survival and creates stress.

In other words, the Human Survival Instinct is hardwired by Nature to fundamentally recognize the world around it as its life-support system.

For this reason, it is 'deathly' afraid of being disconnected from that system.

So, at the core of our being, we humans are unconsciously afraid of not being in relationship with others.

We need our relationships to survive.
We need strong relationships to thrive.

If you want an abundant life filled with Health, Wealth, and Happiness, it's so important that you establish strong and healthy connections with the world around you.

But what is it that makes for a strong and healthy relationship?

- 6 -

GOOD & BAD RELATIONSHIPS

The quality of your life comes down to the balance of two things: Good Relationships and Bad Relationships.

Think of a teeter-totter or a balance scale where you have all your good relationships on one side and all your bad relationships on the other. The way these two sides balance out right now give you a reading of the overall quality of your current life experience.

A GOOD relationship is one that adds to the well-being of those in the relationship.

A BAD relationship takes away from the well-being of those in the relationship.

When you strengthen (add to) another person's well-being, you are strengthening the connection between you. It is a stronger bond that provides a way to exchange more life-energy.

We experience life-energy as feelings of vibrancy, presence, and aliveness.

Strong *connections* (relationships) are vibrant bonds of Trust and Confidence.

When you do something that takes away from someone else's well-being, you have damaged the connection, reduced the Trust, and weakened the bond. Less energy is able to flow between you and so, being together reduces your level of energy.

Good Relationships tend to make you feel great, fill you with energy and excitement.

Bad Relationships tend to make you feel tired, stressed, unhealthy, and worn-out.

So now the remaining question is "How do you create Good Relationships?".

The Foundation of a Good Relationship

Everything I've written so far has been to prepare for this moment. What I'm about to share with you next is the soil in which you will grow Good Relationships.

Every Good Relationship fulfills the fundamental human need of being recognized as valuable by others. People in Good Relationships feel genuinely <u>valued</u> by each other.

Every Bad Relationship neglects this fundamental need and makes the people in them feel less valued.

A Bad Relationship is one that makes you feel less important and worth less. Bad Relationships feel threatening to our Survival Instinct, causing stress and conflict.

Whether a relationship is good or bad depends entirely on whether it fulfills or neglects our basic human need to feel valued by others.

The way to cultivate Good Relationships in your life is to keep this fundamental human need in mind at all times and consistently treat others in a way that makes them feel valued.

What follows now are three simple steps to help you do just that.

- 7 -

STEP ONE:

Set Your Intention to Understand the Other Person.

Y ou now know that the soil in which a Good

Relationship grows is the mutual desire to recognize each other's value.

We call it "Respect".

People feel most valued and respected when their thoughts and feelings are understood and validated.

By consciously setting an intention to genuinely understand the other person, you are literally 'tuning' your brain to organize information in a way that allows you to see their point-of-view as valid. You set the stage to see life through their eyes.

Tuning Your Brain

Your brain has a component called the Reticular Activating System (RAS) that, among its many functions, serves as a filter which determines what you consciously notice and disregard at any given moment.

Your INTENTION plays a key role in setting up this filter.

4x4 Trucks are Suddenly Everywhere

People often notice the effects of their RAS after making important decisions like deciding to buy a new car.

When Fred buys a new Dodge 4x4, he suddenly notices them everywhere and can't believe how many of them are on the road.

He didn't notice them before.

Is everyone copying him?

No. Once Jim set the INTENTION to buy his specific model, his RAS was 'tuned' to notice them because this truck was now a new part of his identity.

Your Amazing Brain Filter

Have you ever been at a party where there's a bunch of people engaged in different conversations at the same time that you were having an interesting conversation with someone else?

The person you were speaking with had your full attention because you were talking about something very interesting.

Even though there were dozens of conversations going on around you, they didn't distract you from your conversation. At least not until.... someone behind you said your name!

Somehow, you managed to hear your name and now your attention has been diverted away from your conversation to focus upon what's being said about you.

How is it that, from the hundreds of different words being uttered at the same time as your conversation, the only outside word you consciously notice is your own name?

This is possible because your brain was actually monitoring every conversation in the room and 'heard' every word but was only 'programmed' to let your name through its (RAS) filter into your conscious attention.

In this case, it was your Survival Instinct that set the INTENTION to notice your name so that you could immediately assess any possible threats.

The Main Point

The main point here is knowing that it is your Intention that has the power to program your brain to automatically find and organize the information you are looking for to bring you to your goal.

Understanding Intention

Intention is <u>not</u> saying what you would *like* to have happen. That would be simply stating a preference.

When you *intend* to do something, you feel **committed** and **determined** to see it through. Your whole being aligns towards fulfilling the intention. There is no room for doubt. Come hell or high water, you will succeed no matter what. This is *Intention*.

If a 'so-called' intention has no commitment or determination attached to it, it is NOT an intention. It is merely a *desire*.

When you set the intention to understand another person, you feel committed and determined to *experience life from <u>their</u> point of view.*

Intentions, like everything else, require the right environment to exist. So, before you can successfully set the intention to truly understand another person's point of view, a few things must first be in place.

You'll need the right mindset.

What follows are four components of the right mindset that support the setting of this intention.

The Right Mindset: *Be Curious and Wonder*

Component A - You Are An Actor

Setting an intention to understand someone else is easily done when you are genuinely curious about what life looks like through their eyes.

One way to generate this curiosity is to pretend that you are an actor and must play the role of this person in an upcoming movie.

It's your job to learn how they think and how they see the world around them.

Component B - You Are Watching A Movie

Another component of the right mindset is to take on the same attitude you have when you decide to watch a movie.

You set your identity down and allow yourself to suspend your disbelief while you allow the movie to take you on a journey.

You don't seek to agree or disagree with anything, you simply allow things to be as they are so that you can genuinely see what life is like from this new vantage point. It's an escape from yourself.

Component C - You Value A Greater Truth

The third component of the right mindset is to recognize that every perspective has value. Every point-of-view has access to information that other points-of-view do not.

No one person's point-of-view can see everything there is to see in the Universe and therefore only has access to a fragment of the whole TRUTH.

There is a small fragment of Truth in every point-of-view. The more points-of-view you allow yourself to see Life from, the more you access a Greater Truth.

Our growth as human-beings depends on us sharing our perspectives and providing each other with access to new information.

We each hold a piece of LIFE's puzzle. For this reason, we are each valuable. We need each other. If someone dies without telling their story, we all lose access to a valuable perspective.

Component D - You Are **Not** Your Point-of-View

The final component of the right mindset for understanding another person's point-of-view is understanding that **you** are <u>not</u> your point-of view and neither is the other person.

You are each a 'Viewer' and can therefore choose which point-of-view you would like to view life from at any given moment.

A point-of-view is simply a place to stand - like on top of a mountain or down in the valley. You are the one who does the standing and the viewing.

That spot on the top of the mountain is not you. Just because you're standing there, doesn't make it 'you'.

STEP 1 - Summary

The first active step in making another person feel valued is to consciously set the Intention to understand their point-of-view. You do this by being naturally curious about what life looks like through their eyes.

This Curious Mindset is supported by the following components:

a) Pretending to be an actor who is learning to play the role of this other person in a movie.

b) Setting your identity aside, releasing the desire to agree or disagree, and simply allowing things to be as they are so you can be taken on a journey to escape yourself for a little while - like when you watch a movie.

c) Understanding that each point-of-view is valuable because it's another fragment of the complete TRUTH. It has a little bit of Truth in it. Look for it. By allowing yourself to see from another's point-of-view, you are gaining access to the Greater Truth.

d) Keeping in mind that you are NOT your point-of-view, you are the Viewer. This means your point-of-view is your choice. You can choose where to view Life from. When you look to understand a new point-of-view, you are expanding your options and your perspective on Life.

Final Note For STEP 1

Being willing to understand another person by taking yourself out of the way sets the stage for

Compassion to arise.

Compassion is the spirit of selflessly caring for another person.

As you share with others your willingness to understand them, they will feel valued and want to keep you in their lives because you help fulfill their fundamental inner need.

They will seek to keep you in their lives by fulfilling your needs in return.

In other words, because you contribute to their well-being, you become valuable to them and, in return, they'll want to add to your well-being.

7

STEP TWO:

Listen With Genuine Interest.

This step is the natural outcropping of Step 1.

As another person is speaking to you, the purpose of being genuinely interested is to help you create rapport and non-verbally communicate that their perspective has value.

Here are a few things you can do to help you genuinely listen more effectively:

Fist of all, pretend to be them as they speak. Again this is an extension from Step 1.

Here you are either pretending to be an actor who is learning to play this person in a movie or you are pretending to be them as you "watch" their movie (picture what they're saying as you listen to them).

Either way, you are essentially standing inside a question that asks, "What would life be like if what this person is saying is true?".

Be curious and open-minded and allow their story to be true as you listen.

Remember that your intention is not to agree or disagree with what you are picturing. You are simply allowing yourself to 'see' in a new way by looking at Life through this new lens.

When you're done, you don't have to keep the lens, you can give it back. However, if you like some of the things you learned through their perspective, you can add this lens to your collection.

Secondly, you can listen for the other person's intention.

Why are they saying what they're saying?

What is it this person wants recognized as valuable?

What is important to them about what they're saying?

Don't answer this question yourself with a bunch of assumptions. Instead, **listen** for the answer. Seek it out.

Remember that we, as people, are always (unconsciously) looking to fulfill our basic need of being recognized as valuable and it fuels the way we speak.

The more a person feels 'heard' and 'understood', the calmer their tone, the safer they feel and the more they open up.

The less a person feels 'heard', the more stressed their tone, the more agitated they feel, and the more they shut down.

These are your indicators.

You know you are on the right track when the other person opens up to you. Discovering how the person speaking to you wants to be recognized as important sets the stage for you to earn their trust.

Thirdly, listen without interrupting and allow the other person to completely finish speaking.

The only time you should speak is to ask the other person a question in order to gain greater clarity about their point-of-view.

When the other person is done speaking they will stop. Count to three silently in your mind and then, if it's appropriate, ask something like, "Is there anything more you'd like to say?".

This question is appropriate when the other person is 'venting' and has something to get off their chest. Otherwise, when they are done speaking, you can ask another question to show interest and further explore their point-of-view or simply move on to step 3.

Finally, only ask questions. Don't make statements unless asked for your input.

This rides the coattails of the last point in that your questions show interest whereas statements of your opinion can often show judgement or disregard for what's been said.

You are looking to **understand** this person. Offering statements of your opinion takes you off-track and changes your mindset from open and curious to one that closes down your understanding of their perspective.

STEP 2 Summary

Listening with genuine interest to another person is incredibly powerful in making them feel valued and respected.

Just think of a time when someone was genuinely interested in what **you** had to say.

How did that make you feel?

But what if someone is talking to you about a subject *they* love but that you find boring, and yet, you still want to grow this relationship?

Simply become curious about what it is exactly they love so much about this topic and then be open to discover the ways in which it adds to their well-being.

Ask, "What do you love most about _____?"

Be the actor learning the role.

Listen for what they want recognized as valuable - this is the intention behind **why** they are saying what they're saying.

Listen without interrupting and don't say a thing unless you are asking a question to help clarify your understanding of their point-of-view.

And finally, listen until they are finished speaking and allow a three second pause of silence to lapse before saying anything else - making sure that the next thing you say is either a question or what's in Step 3.

This pause shows that you are being mindful of what they've said and are taking a moment to process it. You are treating their words as important and valuable.

This pause ...earns their **trust**.

8

STEP THREE

Confirm Your Understanding.

Now that the other person is finished sharing their perspective with you, it's time to find out how well you actually understand their point of view.

You can begin by saying, "So, if I understand you right, you're saying....." and then go on to paraphrase what they've told you using your own words.

Your intention here is to confirm how well you are able to view the world through their eyes.

If they say "Yes, that's exactly what I'm saying!" then congratulations, you've done it!

You've made them feel understood and earned some of their trust.

If they say, "No, that's not what I'm saying." then continue to ask questions and repeat Step 3 by confirming your new understanding with them.

Keep doing this until you get a "Yes!"

Include Their Feelings

Depending on the subject, make sure that you include what you understand about how this person feels about what they were talking about.

Were they upset? excited? nervous? happy?

If you've done a good job listening to them from *their* point-of-view, you will have felt the same emotion they felt as they were speaking.

It's just like when you watch movie - when you are truly engaged, you will feel the emotions the movie's characters are expressing.

Commenting on noticing their feelings helps validate that it was okay for them to feel what they felt.

Please note that it is okay for people to feel what they feel even if you don't agree with their emotional reaction.

Our feelings come from our perception. Our points-of-view naturally limit what information we perceive. If another person felt something that you think is a bit extreme, it's a sign that you didn't completely see the world through their eyes. You're still viewing from your old perspective.

If you surrendered your point-of-view (like when you watch a movie) and accessed the exact same information as this person, you would be able to understand how they could feel what they felt.

Validating another person's feelings is a silent way of saying that they are okay just the way they are. Their feelings didn't come from "them", their feelings came from their point-of-view; from where they were standing and viewing Life.

People aren't their points-of-view and so it is unfair to judge them for experiencing the feelings that their points-of-view offered them.

Most people never realize they are a 'Viewer'. They think they **are** their point-of-view and sadly, as a result, never realize that the way they view Life can actually be a choice.

Always keep in mind that there is a big difference between viewing from another person's perspective and agreeing with it.

To view the world from another person's perspective is to explore a new vantage point.

To agree with another person's point of view (opinion) is to choose it as *your* primary point-of-view on the subject too.

Remember, just because you visit a place, doesn't mean you have to live there.

Your inner 'home' is made from all the points-of-view you enjoy living from.

Understanding another person is like visiting them in their home-land and getting a personal tour.

While in their home-land, you will seek to understand their customs.

Once you return 'home' (the conversation ends), you can take with you whatever customs you liked and simply discard the rest.

You do not have to *live* in another person's home-land to understand them and create a deeper connection with them. You need only visit.

Enjoy your travels and all the treasures you'll find.

9

YOUR CHALLENGE – YOUR BENEFITS

Think about the relationships you have right now in your life with family, friends, acquaintances, and co-workers.

If any conflict ever arose between you and one of them, it was likely because one or both of you felt undervalued or disrespected by the other.

It's time for a change - one that will strengthen every relationship that you consistently apply these three steps to.

What I'm about to ask you to do will take strength but I promise you that your benefits will far outweigh your effort.

You'll get a great return on your investment.

The Challenge

I invite you now to go out and be willing to
understand other people **first** in spite of
whether or not they are willing to understand
you.

Most conflicts arise from both sides asserting
their need to be understood while, at the same
time, being unwilling to first understand the
other.

Both sides are taking and no-one is giving. It's a
tug-of-war. Nothing can be resolved when this
happens. One person has to be first. Let that
person be you. You be the change-agent.

When you seek to understand someone ***before***
expecting them to understand you, you
generate the spirit of 'being heard'.

This is compassion.

Once someone feels genuinely understood, more often than not, they will want to hear what you have to say.

It's like the old adage: "No-one cares how much you know until they know how much you care".

The Benefits

As you do this consistently, you grow more trust in your life and people grow to love you more.

Remember that trust is the indicator of a strengthened connection between you.

Building an environment of trust provides a greater sense of ease and relaxation in your daily affairs. You'll have less stress and things will run smoother.

In this environment, your Health, Wealth, and Happiness can only improve.

As you set the intention to grow your income, opportunities will naturally present themselves more often because of the trust you've developed. More people will want to work with you because they feel heard by you. They feel valued. You will earn a solid reputation as someone who is great to work with.

By consistently being willing to listen before you speak and seeking to understand before being understood, you create and sustain the environment that supports a beautiful life.

Now go for it!

- 10 -

A New Vision

Thank you for investing in reading this book.

I know that if you choose to apply what I've shared with you here, you will fall more in love with life.

Just imagine...

If the whole world practiced the principles in this book, what do you suppose the world would be like?

Here is my vision:

I see a world filled with people who are willing to understand one another.

It is a world where we recognize the wisdom of Diversity and realize that it is our differences that sustain life. It's in these differences that we find and meet each other's needs.

We recognize that "Same-ness" cannot bring about growth. We are the living balance of Unity in Diversity. We are free to be ourselves.

I see a world without war or conflict; a world without guns or the need to defend anything because the people of the world share a common mindset.

We see the ways in which we are all part of the one environment that sustains us.

Everyone knows that to harm someone else is like pouring poison into the garden of life that feeds us. We know that in bringing harm, we poison our own lives.

We live in peace. Rather, we live in Harmony. Harmony is a state where everyone sings their own note and all the notes fit together to form something that sounds beautiful and strengthens all.

Each note in Harmony adds beauty.

I see a world of abundance. This is a world free of starvation because we find more value in each other than we do in money.

We realize that people are the real currency of life and investing in each other is the best investment we can make.

The return on this investment is immeasurably high because everything we do is for our mutual benefit.

A rising tide raises all ships and this tide of mutual benefit creates abundance for all. It sets the stage for incredible advancements in science, technology, art, music, health, and recreation.

We live with great passion and appreciation for life.

I see a world I want to live in and proudly give to future generations.

You Are Power

As you practice the 3 Steps in this book, your way of being expands the environment that supports this vision.

YOU are the essential element in how this world changes. Your conscious intention to enhance your relationships inspires others to do the same.

As more people practice this process, our world inevitably becomes more and more like the one described above.

Please share what you've learned here with others and use it daily. When you do, you are part of a movement growing toward the tipping point where mutual respect becomes common practice. When it does, it will be the dawn of a new and exciting world that YOU have helped create.

I envision a world where we are all looking out for each other.

Thank you again so much for reading this book.

I value the difference that your presence makes.

It is the power you are.

– Trent Janisch

About the Author

Trent Janisch is a personal development coach working internationally with private clients. He also develops and facilitates transformational training programs for corporations and live public events.

Trent views what he calls 'Natural Hypnosis' as the cause of much human suffering. He says,

"Many people have fallen asleep to the power they are. They've been unknowingly hypnotized into a type of blindness that keeps them from seeing their own powerful influence upon the world around them. My intention is to help you live a better life by having you recognize the power of your own presence and then to use it wisely to consciously shape your own life."

Trent is happily married and lives with his family in British Columbia, Canada.

You can contact the author by visiting www.trentjanisch.com.

ADDITIONAL RESOURCES

Be Part of a Growing Community

If you enjoyed this book and would like to know more about developing your relationship skills, resilience, influence, and consciously shaping your own life, please join my mailing list at **trentjanisch.com** and stay current with the latest updates, free downloads, special offers, and event announcements. I look forward to getting to know you.

Coaching for Success

Creating change in your life (like applying the steps in this book) can be challenging.

The reason is, while you may already know *what* you need to do in order to change your life for the better, you may not know exactly *how* to make this knowledge part of your *consistent daily routine* at home or at work.

Creating change can be difficult because you have within you an automatic system of habits that work together to hold each other in place.

When you attempt to create a new consistent behaviour, your habit-system perceives it as a threat and resists your efforts. As a result, the new behaviour feels uncomfortable and you return to your old life-pattern. Hence, nothing changes.

If this is you, don't lose hope! The right coaching can help you break free of those old patterns and develop the lifestyle you really want.

Come visit me at **trentjanisch.com** and see how good coaching can positively change your life.

I'm here to help.

Thank you, again, for reading this book.

May your life be blessed.

Made in the USA
Charleston, SC
29 December 2016